www.providencebooks.net

Publisher Contact

Email:contact@providencebooks.net

Social media: facebook.com/providencebooks

Acknowledgements

The team at Providence Books would like to thank our friends, family, suppliers and customers for making our vision of creating the highest-quality books a reality. Thanks for purchasing and enjoy the quotes!

This page is intentionally left blank

This page is intentionally left blank

A countryman between two lawyers is like a fish between two cats.

Benjamin Franklin

A good conscience is a continual Christmas.

Benjamin Franklin

A great empire, like a great cake, is most easily diminished at the edges.

Benjamin Franklin

A house is not a home unless it contains food and fire for the mind as well as the body.

Benjamin Franklin

A learned blockhead is a greater blockhead than an ignorant one.

Benjamin Franklin

A life of leisure and a life of laziness are two things. There will be sleeping enough in the grave.

Benjamin Franklin

A man wrapped up in himself makes a very small bundle.

Benjamin Franklin

A penny saved is a penny earned.

Benjamin Franklin

A place for everything, everything in its place.

Benjamin Franklin

Admiration is the daughter of ignorance.

Benjamin Franklin

All mankind is divided into three classes: those that are immovable, those that are movable, and those that move.

Benjamin Franklin

All wars are follies, very expensive and very mischievous ones.

Benjamin Franklin

All who think cannot but see there is a sanction like that of religion which binds us in partnership in the serious work of the world.

Benjamin Franklin

An investment in knowledge pays the best interest.

Benjamin Franklin

And whether you're an honest man, or whether you're a thief, depends on whose solicitor has given me my brief.

Benjamin Franklin

Anger is never without a reason, but seldom with a good one.

Benjamin Franklin

Any fool can criticize, condemn and complain - and most fools do.

Benjamin Franklin

Applause waits on success.

Benjamin Franklin

As we must account for every idle word, so must we account for every idle silence.

Benjamin Franklin

At twenty years of age the will reigns; at thirty, the wit; and at forty, the judgment.

Benjamin Franklin

Be at war with your vices, at peace with your neighbors, and let every new year find you a better man.

Benjamin Franklin

Be slow in choosing a friend, slower in changing.

Benjamin Franklin

Beauty and folly are old companions.

Benjamin Franklin

Being ignorant is not so much a shame, as being unwilling to learn.

Benjamin Franklin

Beware of little expenses. A small leak will sink a great ship.

Benjamin Franklin

Beware the hobby that eats.

Benjamin Franklin

Buy what thou hast no need of and ere long thou shalt sell thy necessities.

Benjamin Franklin

By failing to prepare, you are preparing to fail.

Benjamin Franklin

Content makes poor men rich; discontent makes rich men poor.

Benjamin Franklin

Creditors have better memories than debtors.

Benjamin Franklin

Diligence is the mother of good luck.

Benjamin Franklin

Distrust and caution are the parents of security.

Benjamin Franklin

Do good to your friends to keep them, to your enemies to win them.

Benjamin Franklin

Do not fear mistakes. You will know failure. Continue to reach out.

Benjamin Franklin

Dost thou love life? Then do not squander time, for that is the stuff life is made of.

Benjamin Franklin

Each year one vicious habit discarded, in time might make the worst of us good.

Benjamin Franklin

Early to bed and early to rise makes a man healthy, wealthy and wise.

Benjamin Franklin

Eat to please thyself, but dress to please others.

Benjamin Franklin

Either write something worth reading or do something worth writing.

Benjamin Franklin

Employ thy time well, if thou meanest to gain leisure.

Benjamin Franklin

Energy and persistence conquer all things.

Benjamin Franklin

Even peace may be purchased at too high a price.

Benjamin Franklin

Experience keeps a dear school, but fools will learn in no other.

Benjamin Franklin

Fatigue is the best pillow.

Benjamin Franklin

For having lived long, I have experienced many instances of being obliged, by better information or fuller consideration, to change opinions, even on important subjects, which I once thought right but found to be otherwise.

Benjamin Franklin

Gain may be temporary and uncertain; but ever while you live, expense is constant and certain: and it is easier to build two chimneys than to keep one in fuel.

Benjamin Franklin

Games lubricate the body and the mind.

Benjamin Franklin

Genius without education is like silver in the mine.

Benjamin Franklin

God helps those who help themselves.

Benjamin Franklin

God works wonders now and then; Behold a lawyer, an honest man.

Benjamin Franklin

Guests, like fish, begin to smell after three days.

Benjamin Franklin

Half a truth is often a great lie.

Benjamin Franklin

Having been poor is no shame, but being ashamed of it, is.

Benjamin Franklin

He does not possess wealth; it possesses him.

Benjamin Franklin

He that can have patience can have what he will.

Benjamin Franklin

He that composes himself is wiser than he that composes a book.

Benjamin Franklin

He that displays too often his wife and his wallet is in danger of having both of them borrowed.

Benjamin Franklin

He that has done you a kindness will be more ready to do you another, than he whom you yourself have obliged.

Benjamin Franklin

He that is good for making excuses is seldom good for anything else.

Benjamin Franklin

He that is of the opinion money will do everything may well be suspected of doing everything for money.

Benjamin Franklin

He that lives upon hope will die fasting.

Benjamin Franklin

He that raises a large family does, indeed, while he lives to observe them, stand a broader mark for sorrow; but then he stands a broader mark for pleasure too.

Benjamin Franklin

He that rises late must trot all day.

Benjamin Franklin

He that speaks much, is much mistaken.

Benjamin Franklin

He that waits upon fortune, is never sure of a dinner.

Benjamin Franklin

He that won't be counseled can't be helped.

Benjamin Franklin

He that would live in peace and at ease must not speak all he knows or all he sees.

Benjamin Franklin

He that's secure is not safe.

Benjamin Franklin

He who falls in love with himself will have no rivals.

Benjamin Franklin

Hear reason, or she'll make you feel her.

Benjamin Franklin

Hide not your talents. They for use were made. What's a sundial in the shade?

Benjamin Franklin

Honesty is the best policy.

Benjamin Franklin

How few there are who have courage enough to own their faults, or resolution enough to mend them.

Benjamin Franklin

Human felicity is produced not as much by great pieces of good fortune that seldom happen as by little advantages that occur every day.

Benjamin Franklin

Hunger is the best pickle.

Benjamin Franklin

I am for doing good to the poor, but I differ in opinion about the means. I think the best way of doing good to the poor is not making them easy in poverty, but leading or driving them out of it.

Benjamin Franklin

I conceive that the great part of the miseries of mankind are brought upon them by false estimates they have made of the value of things.

Benjamin Franklin

I didn't fail the test, I just found 100 ways to do it wrong.

Benjamin Franklin

I guess I don't so much mind being old, as I mind being fat and old.

Benjamin Franklin

I look upon death to be as necessary to our constitution as sleep. We shall rise refreshed in the morning.

Benjamin Franklin

I saw few die of hunger; of eating, a hundred thousand.

Benjamin Franklin

I should have no objection to go over the same life from its beginning to the end: requesting only the advantage authors have, of correcting in a second edition the faults of the first.

Benjamin Franklin

I wake up every morning at nine and grab for the morning paper. Then I look at the obituary page. If my name is not on it, I get up.

Benjamin Franklin

If a man could have half of his wishes, he would double his troubles.

Benjamin Franklin

If a man empties his purse into his head, no one can take it from him.

Benjamin Franklin

If all printers were determined not to print anything till they were sure it would offend nobody, there would be very little printed.

Benjamin Franklin

If passion drives you, let reason hold the reins.

Benjamin Franklin

If time be of all things the most precious, wasting time must be the greatest prodigality.

Benjamin Franklin

If we do not hang together, we shall surely hang separately.

Benjamin Franklin

If you desire many things, many things will seem few.

Benjamin Franklin

If you know how to spend less than you get, you have the philosopher's stone.

Benjamin Franklin

If you would be loved, love, and be loveable.

Benjamin Franklin

If you would have a faithful servant, and one that you like, serve yourself.

Benjamin Franklin

If you would know the value of money, go and try to borrow some.

Benjamin Franklin

If you would not be forgotten as soon as you are dead, either write something worth reading or do things worth writing.

Benjamin Franklin

In general, mankind, since the improvement of cookery, eats twice as much as nature requires.

Benjamin Franklin

In my youth, I traveled much, and I observed in different countries, that the more public provisions were made for the poor, the less they provided for themselves, and of course became poorer. And, on the contrary, the less was done for them, the more they did for themselves, and became richer.

Benjamin Franklin

In the affairs of this world, men are saved not by faith, but by the want of it.

Benjamin Franklin

In this world nothing can be said to be certain, except death and taxes.

Benjamin Franklin

Industry need not wish.

Benjamin Franklin

It is a grand mistake to think of being great without goodness and I pronounce it as certain that there was never a truly great man that was not at the same time truly virtuous.

Benjamin Franklin

It is easier to prevent bad habits than to break them.

Benjamin Franklin

It is much easier to suppress a first desire than to satisfy those that follow.

Benjamin Franklin

It is only when the rich are sick that they fully feel the impotence of wealth.

Benjamin Franklin

It is the eye of other people that ruin us. If I were blind I would want, neither fine clothes, fine houses or fine furniture.

Benjamin Franklin

It is the working man who is the happy man. It is the idle man who is the miserable man.

Benjamin Franklin

It takes many good deeds to build a good reputation, and only one bad one to lose it.

Benjamin Franklin

Keep your eyes wide open before marriage, half shut afterwards.

Benjamin Franklin

Laws too gentle are seldom obeyed; too severe, seldom executed.

Benjamin Franklin

Leisure is the time for doing something useful. This leisure the diligent person will obtain the lazy one never.

Benjamin Franklin

Life's Tragedy is that we get old to soon and wise too late.

Benjamin Franklin

Lost time is never found again.

Benjamin Franklin

Many a man thinks he is buying pleasure, when he is really selling himself to it.

Benjamin Franklin

Many foxes grow gray but few grow good.

Benjamin Franklin

Many people die at twenty five and aren't buried until they are seventy five.

Benjamin Franklin

Marriage is the most natural state of man, and... the state in which you will find solid happiness.

Benjamin Franklin

Mine is better than ours.

Benjamin Franklin

Money has never made man happy, nor will it, there is nothing in its nature to produce happiness. The more of it one has the more one wants.

Benjamin Franklin

Most people return small favors, acknowledge medium ones and repay greater ones - with ingratitude.

Benjamin Franklin

Necessity never made a good bargain.

Benjamin Franklin

Never confuse motion with action.

Benjamin Franklin

Never leave that till tomorrow which you can do today.

Benjamin Franklin

Never take a wife till thou hast a house (and a fire) to put her in.

Benjamin Franklin

Nine men in ten are would be suicides.

Benjamin Franklin

No nation was ever ruined by trade.

Benjamin Franklin

Observe all men, thyself most.

Benjamin Franklin

One today is worth two tomorrows.

Benjamin Franklin

Our necessities never equal our wants.

Benjamin Franklin

Rather go to bed with out dinner than to rise in debt.

Benjamin Franklin

Rebellion against tyrants is obedience to God.

Benjamin Franklin

Remember not only to say the right thing in the right place, but far more difficult still, to leave unsaid the wrong thing at the tempting moment.

Benjamin Franklin

Remember that credit is money.

Benjamin Franklin

Savages we call them because their manners differ from ours.

Benjamin Franklin

She laughs at everything you say. Why? Because she has fine teeth.

Benjamin Franklin

Since thou are not sure of a minute, throw not away an hour.

Benjamin Franklin

Some people die at 25 and aren't buried until 75.

Benjamin Franklin

Speak ill of no man, but speak all the good you know of everybody.

Benjamin Franklin

Take time for all things: great haste makes great waste.

Benjamin Franklin

Tell me and I forget. Teach me and I remember. Involve me and I learn.

Benjamin Franklin

The Constitution only gives people the right to pursue happiness. You have to catch it yourself.

Benjamin Franklin

The U. S. Constitution doesn't guarantee happiness, only the pursuit of it. You have to catch up with it yourself.

Benjamin Franklin

The absent are never without fault, nor the present without excuse.

Benjamin Franklin

The art of acting consists in keeping people from coughing.

Benjamin Franklin

The discontented man finds no easy chair.

Benjamin Franklin

The doors of wisdom are never shut.

Benjamin Franklin

The doorstep to the temple of wisdom is a knowledge of our own ignorance.

Benjamin Franklin

The eye of the master will do more work than both his hands.

Benjamin Franklin

The first mistake in public business is the going into it.

Benjamin Franklin

The strictest law sometimes becomes the severest injustice.

Benjamin Franklin

The use of money is all the advantage there is in having it.

Benjamin Franklin

The way to see by Faith is to shut the Eye of Reason.

Benjamin Franklin

The worst wheel of the cart makes the most noise.

Benjamin Franklin

There are three faithful friends - an old wife, an old dog, and ready money.

Benjamin Franklin

There are three things extremely hard: steel, a diamond, and to know one's self.

Benjamin Franklin

There are two ways of being happy: We must either diminish our wants or augment our means - either may do - the result is the same and it is for each man to decide for himself and to do that which happens to be easier.

Benjamin Franklin

There is no kind of dishonesty into which otherwise good people more easily and frequently fall than that of defrauding the government.

Benjamin Franklin

There never was a truly great man that was not at the same time truly virtuous.

Benjamin Franklin

There was never a good war, or a bad peace.

Benjamin Franklin

They who can give up essential liberty to obtain a little temporary safety deserve neither liberty nor safety.

Benjamin Franklin

Those disputing, contradicting, and confuting people are generally unfortunate in their affairs. They get victory, sometimes, but they never get good will, which would be of more use to them.

Benjamin Franklin

Those that won't be counseled can't be helped.

Benjamin Franklin

Those who govern, having much business on their hands, do not generally like to take the trouble of considering and carrying into execution new projects. The best public measures are therefore seldom adopted from previous wisdom, but forced by the occasion.

Benjamin Franklin

Three can keep a secret, if two of them are dead.

Benjamin Franklin

Time is money.

Benjamin Franklin

To Follow by faith alone is to follow blindly.

Benjamin Franklin

To lengthen thy life, lessen thy meals.

Benjamin Franklin

To succeed, jump as quickly at opportunities as you do at conclusions.

Benjamin Franklin

Tomorrow, every Fault is to be amended; but that Tomorrow never comes.

Benjamin Franklin

Tricks and treachery are the practice of fools, that don't have brains enough to be honest.

Benjamin Franklin

Trouble springs from idleness, and grievous toil from needless ease.

Benjamin Franklin

Wars are not paid for in wartime, the bill comes later.

Benjamin Franklin

We are all born ignorant, but one must work hard to remain stupid.

Benjamin Franklin

We are more thoroughly an enlightened people, with respect to our political interests, than perhaps any other under heaven. Every man among us reads, and is so easy in his circumstances as to have leisure for conversations of improvement and for acquiring information.

Benjamin Franklin

We must, indeed, all hang together or, most assuredly, we shall all hang separately.

Benjamin Franklin

Wealth is not his that has it, but his that enjoys it.

Benjamin Franklin

Well done is better than well said.

Benjamin Franklin

Whatever is begun in anger ends in shame.

Benjamin Franklin

When befriended, remember it; when you befriend, forget it.

Benjamin Franklin

When in doubt, don't.

Benjamin Franklin

When men and woman die, as poets sung, his heart's the last part moves, her last, the tongue.

Benjamin Franklin

When will mankind be convinced and agree to settle their difficulties by arbitration?

Benjamin Franklin

When you're finished changing, you're finished.

Benjamin Franklin

Where liberty is, there is my country.

Benjamin Franklin

Where sense is wanting, everything is wanting.

Benjamin Franklin

Where there's marriage without love, there will be love without marriage.

Benjamin Franklin

Who had deceived thee so often as thyself?

Benjamin Franklin

Who is rich? He that is content. Who is that? Nobody.

Benjamin Franklin

Who is rich? He that rejoices in his portion.

Benjamin Franklin

Who is wise? He that learns from everyone. Who is powerful? He that governs his passions. Who is rich? He that is content. Who is that? Nobody.

Benjamin Franklin

Wine is constant proof that God loves us and loves to see us happy.

Benjamin Franklin

Wise men don't need advice. Fools won't take it.

Benjamin Franklin

Without continual growth and progress, such words as improvement, achievement, and success have no meaning.

Benjamin Franklin

Words may show a man's wit but actions his meaning.

Benjamin Franklin

Work as if you were to live a hundred years. Pray as if you were to die tomorrow.

Benjamin Franklin

Write injuries in dust, benefits in marble.

Benjamin Franklin

Write your injuries in dust, your benefits in marble.

Benjamin Franklin

You can bear your own faults, and why not a fault in your wife?

Benjamin Franklin

You may delay, but time will not.

Benjamin Franklin

Your net worth to the world is usually determined by what remains after your bad habits are subtracted from your good ones.

Benjamin Franklin

This page is intentionally left blank

This page is intentionally left blank

This page is intentionally left blank

This page is intentionally left blank

This page is intentionally left blank

www.ingramcontent.com/pod-product-compliance
Lightning Source LLC
Chambersburg PA
CBHW071144280526
45787CB00003B/1400